The Wonder of
KANGAROOS

To my now-grown son, Kyle, who was once a kyle-a-roo

— Judith Logan Lehne

Please visit our web site at: www.garethstevens.com
For a free color catalog describing Gareth Stevens Publishing's list of high-quality books
and multimedia programs, call 1-800-542-2595 (USA) or 1-800-461-9120 (Canada).
Gareth Stevens Publishing's Fax: (414) 332-3567.

Library of Congress Cataloging-in-Publication Data available upon request from publisher.
Fax: (414) 336-0157 for the attention of the Publishing Records Department.

ISBN 0-8368-2766-X

First published in North America in 2001 by
Gareth Stevens Publishing
A World Almanac Education Group Company
330 West Olive Street, Suite 100
Milwaukee, WI 53212 USA

This edition is based on the book *Kangaroos for Kids,* text © 1997 by Judith Logan Lehne, with
illustrations by John F. McGee, first published in the United States in 1997 by NorthWord Press,
(Creative Publishing international, Inc.), Minnetonka, MN, and published as *Kangaroo Magic for
Kids* in a library edition by Gareth Stevens, Inc., in 2000. Additional end matter © 2001 by
Gareth Stevens, Inc.

Photographs © 1997: Hans Reinhard/Bruce Coleman, Inc.: Cover; Jen and Des Bartlett/Bruce
Coleman, Inc.: 15, 20-21, 47; Tom DiMauro/The Wildlife Collection: 6; Martin Harvey/The
Wildlife Collection: 8, 10-11, 18, 30-31, 40, 44; John Giustina/The Wildlife Collection: 14;
Martin Withers/Dembinsky Photo Associates: 16-17; Art Wolfe: 23, 34, 39; Chris Huss/The
Wildlife Collection: 26; Gavriel Jecan/Art Wolfe, Inc.: 28; Len Rue, Jr./Bruce Coleman, Inc.: 32;
Joe McDonald/Bruce Coleman, Inc.: 36-37; Norman Owen Tomalin/Bruce Coleman, Inc.: 42-43.

Printed in the United States of America

1 2 3 4 5 6 7 8 9 05 04 03 02 01

The Wonder of
KANGAROOS

by Patricia Lantier and Judith Logan Lehne
Illustrations by John F. McGee

Gareth Stevens Publishing
A WORLD ALMANAC EDUCATION GROUP COMPANY

Late at night,
while you are
asleep, you
probably will
not have
kangaroos
hopping
around
outside
your house.
But people
in Australia
sometimes do!

Australia has more kangaroos than it has people. A kangaroo is a mammal that carries its babies in a pouch on its belly.

red kangaroos

There are more than sixty species of kangaroos. They all come from Australia and its nearby islands.

Wallabies are part of the kangaroo family. Wallaroos are, too. They are marsupials. They all have a pouch.

swamp wallaby

When English explorers asked about these animals, aborigines answered, "Kangaroo!" which means "I don't understand."

gray kangaroos

Red kangaroos and gray kangaroos are the biggest of the species. Some male kangaroos can grow more than 7 feet (2 meters) tall and can weigh more than 200 pounds (90 kilograms). That's about the same size as some professional basketball players!

Wallaroos are smaller than red or gray kangaroos. Wallabies are even smaller than wallaroos.

common wallaroo

A kangaroo's soft, woolly fur
can be many different colors —
red, gray, brown, or silver.

Red kangaroos can hop as fast as 30 miles (48 kilometers) per hour and leap more than 6 feet (2 m) high. Their large hind legs and back feet are specially built for hopping.

red kangaroo

Tree kangaroos hop, too. They will jump as far as 30 feet (9 m) between trees, looking for a meal.

Although hopping takes a lot of energy, kangaroos can hop all day long!

Kangaroos use their lightning speed and long leaps to escape danger.

red kangaroo

As they hop, kangaroos use their long tails to keep their balance. They also rest on their strong tails — using them as built-in chairs!

Sometimes kangaroos lie on their sides. They like to nap in the afternoon sun.

Although they don't enjoy it, kangaroos can swim, too.

If there is no other
way to escape danger,
they paddle to safety.

Kangaroos are nocturnal animals, which means they are active mostly at night.

gray kangaroo

During the hot day, kangaroos
rest in cool, shady places. They
pant, sweat, and lick their arms
to keep cool.

Most kangaroos are plant eaters,
or herbivores. They mostly eat
grass and the leaves of trees.

Their teeth are designed to chew their food thoroughly. The front teeth, called incisors, cut the plants. Their back teeth, called molars, chew and grind the food.

The plants kangaroos eat are coarse and tough. They often bring up swallowed food to chew it again.

gray kangaroo

Because kangaroos get water from the plants they eat, they can go for months without drinking water.

Kangaroos have terrific eyesight, which makes hopping at night easy.

Kangaroos can also hear very well. Their ears move to hear sounds coming from different directions.

Kangaroos must see and hear well to keep safe. People and dingoes are their biggest enemies, but other animals also prey on them.

red kangaroo

To "talk" to each other,
kangaroos hiss, cough,
cluck, click their tongues,
and even touch each other.

Before
a female
kangaroo
has a
baby, she
cleans
out her
pouch.
A baby
kangaroo
is called
a joey.

red kangaroo

gray kangaroo joey

When a joey is born, it climbs into its mother's pouch for food and safety. It takes up to 30 minutes to climb about 6 inches (15 centimeters). That is a very long way for a baby the size of a bee!

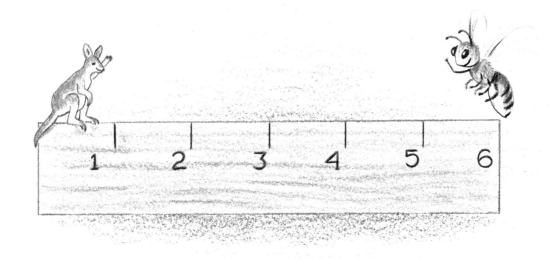

When it is
very young,
the joey stays
safely inside
its mother's
pouch. At
six months
old, the joey
leaves the
pouch for a
few minutes
each day.

red kangaroos

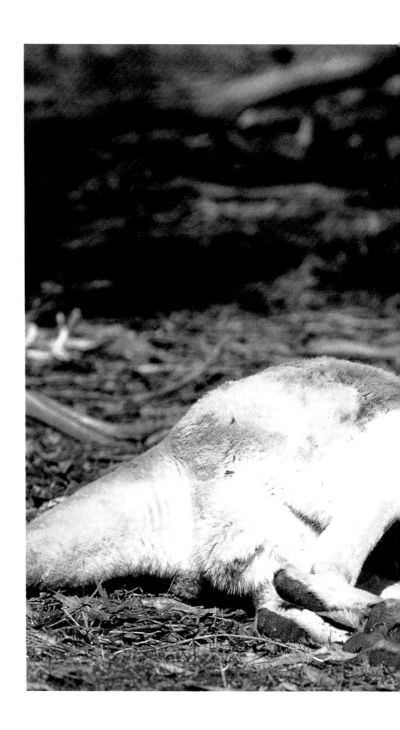

red kangaroos

As joeys grow bigger and stronger, they learn how to defend themselves by boxing and wrestling with older kangaroos. They learn to claw, punch, and kick.

But kangaroos are usually gentle creatures. They would much rather hop away than fight.

Kangaroos are amazing and beautiful animals. If you ever visit Australia, you will surely see them, especially at night.

Sometimes in Australia, when you should be asleep, you might even see kangaroos hopping around outside. But don't stay up too long. You should get hopping into bed!

Glossary

aborigines — the native people of Australia

dingoes — wild dogs in Australia

habitat — the place where certain animals and plants live in nature

incisors — the front teeth that cut food

mammals — warm-blooded animals that feed their young with mother's milk

marsupials — mammals that have a pouch on their abdomen in which to nurse and carry their young

molars — the wide, flat back teeth that grind and chew food

prey (v) — to hunt and eat animals for food

species — a group of animals or plants with similar characteristics

Index